3.99 0
428.6
KET
(D22)

First I win a contest that
makes me a TV star.
Then I get to do some of
the most awesome extreme
sports in the world. And my
two best friends get
to come along for the ride.
How lucky am I?

First published in Great Britain in 2005 by
RISING STARS UK LTD.
76 Farnaby Road, Bromley, BR1 4BH

First published in Australia by Scholastic Australia in 2004.
Text copyright © Philip Kettle, 2004.

A Black Hills book, produced by black dog books

Designed by Blue Boat Design
Cover photo: Blue Boat Design

For more information visit our website at:
www.risingstars-uk.com

British Library Cataloguing in Publication Data

A CIP record for this book is available from the British Library.

ISBN 1 905056 41 9

Printed by Bookmarque Ltd, Croydon, Surrey

# THE Xtreme WORLD OF BILLY KOOL

by Phil Kettle

book:02
whitewater rafting

RISING STARS

# CONTENTS

# WHITEWATER RAFTING EQUIPMENT

### Wetsuit Boots
Wetsuit boots are worn to keep you from slipping over in the raft or on rocks.

### Life Jacket
A life jacket will keep you afloat if you fall out of the raft.

### Drybag
A drybag will keep all your things, such as food and thermal blankets, dry.

### Straps
Straps are used to lash gear to the frame of the raft to stop things falling out.

### Rescue Bag
A rescue bag has 20 metres of rope in it and is thrown to anyone who may fall out.

### Whitewater Raft
These rafts are made out of Hypalon or laminated PVC, which are both very sturdy.

### Paddles
Paddles are used to steer and propel the raft.

### Neoprene Gloves
Neoprene gloves will keep your hands warm and give you a good grip.

### Helmet
A helmet will protect your head from rocks and overhanging branches.

MY FRENCH TEACHER

Lots of things have changed since the first episode of *The Xtreme World of Billy Kool* has been on television. Even though it wasn't a show with an extreme sport in it (it was about how a TV show gets made), Nathan and I had gone from being called little nerds by the older kids at school, to being called lucky little nerds.

Nathan's older sister Crystal, who is the hottest girl I've ever seen, called me by name for the first time ever.

Sally said that one of the boys in the class above us had told her that he liked her. Nathan told Sally that he was way too old for her and that he was really funny looking anyway!

Mum and Dad seemed to be checking on me even more than they normally did. They kept making sure that I was doing all my homework—especially my French homework. Some things never change. Mum and Dad were constantly threatening to stop my television show if my schoolwork suffered. There was no way I was going to let that happen!

I wanted to do extreme sports, even if butterflies were whitewater rafting in my stomach. More than that, I wanted to be really good at them.

Sometimes when I was sitting in class I found it really hard to concentrate on what I was supposed to be learning, particularly on Wednesday afternoons!

On Wednesday afternoons we had French lessons. Our teacher was Mrs Crabtree. Having a name like Mrs Crabtree and being a teacher was bad enough. But having a name like Mrs Crabtree and teaching the worst subject that had ever been invented was even worse.

French. I could never work out why it was important to learn any language other than English.

Surely it would be a lot better if everybody in the world just spoke English.

Instead of having to listen to Mrs Crabtree trying to teach French to our class for two hours each week, we could be outside playing basketball. That would be much more fun!

I was sitting at my desk debating these questions with myself when there was gentle tap on my shoulder.

'Billy, have you been listening to what I've been saying?'

I nearly jumped out of my seat. I could feel my face getting hot and red.

'Yes ... ah, I think so,' I said, not knowing what I should be saying.

'Stay back after class, Billy,' Mrs Crabtree said. 'You and I had better have a little talk about the importance and the benefits of learning to speak French!'

I stayed back after class. Mrs Crabtree, with her index finger waving at me, explained how important learning French really was. I didn't say much. Occasionally I nodded my head in agreement with her. I figured that if I said anything at all, it might only extend the time that I had to stay in the classroom.

Eventually, after what seemed like forever, Mrs Crabtree said that I could go. I promised that I would try harder and I kind of meant it too. At least, I was going to try and find a really good reason why I should like French!

THE MONSTER

Sally and Nathan were waiting for me at the school gate. We walked home from school together every day.

We always had a small extreme moment on the way home. We had to walk past the home of the monster. The monster lived in a back garden behind a two-metre tin fence.

We had never seen the entire monster. This added to the mystery.

In the last year the monster had made a gutter at the bottom of the fence by constantly running along the fence line. We could now see its feet. They might have been the feet of a lion. That's how big they were!

We banged on the fence. The monster erupted with growls and roars that frightened us more than whitewater rafting ever could. We ran down the road. Sally said that one day the monster was going to come straight through the fence and turn the three of us into his next dinner.

Opposite the fence is a park, where every kid in the neighbourhood plays cricket. The best batters always try to hit balls over the monster's fence. Nathan said he reckoned that there would have to be at least a hundred cricket balls behind the fence. 'One day, I'm going to get over that fence and get those balls.'

'Yeah right,' Sally and I said.

We were nearly home when I finished telling Nathan and Sally my theory about the entire world speaking the same language. Sally stopped. We both turned and looked at her.

She waved her index finger around, pretending to be Mrs Crabtree. 'Billy, if all the birds in the world sang the same song, how boring do you think the world would be?' Then she turned back into Sally and started walking away. 'I'll meet you at the tree house in half an hour,' she said, over her shoulder.

Well, of course that was the end of my theory. But I guess if all the birds in the world were like the parrot that we had at home it would be pretty interesting. Wow, what a thought. Magpies sitting in trees, not whistling, but saying 'Polly wants a cracker.'

ARE WE MATURE?

The top of Sally's head appeared at the entrance of our tree house. Nathan and I were lying on the floor, with our chins over the edge.

'You boys are disgusting,' said Sally as she climbed into the tree house.

'What makes you think we're disgusting?' I asked.

'Well,' said Sally, 'we have our own TV show and you and Nathan are dropping spit into ant holes!'

'We're just giving the ants an extreme test of their water survival skills,' said Nathan.

I was sure that Nathan was disappointed when Sally said anything negative about him.

'I'd hardly say that what you're dropping out of your mouths is even close to water — it's more like poison!' she said.

'The ants might be feeling like we'll be feeling this weekend — very nervous,' I said.

'Yeah, when we're going down the rapids and under waterfalls, it might feel exactly the same,' said Nathan.

'But at least we'll be getting drenched by water and not spit—

that's a big difference,' said Sally.

'At least there are no TV cameras
here recording everything that we
do. Anyway, I can remember you
doing the same thing last year,' I
said to Sally.

'That was ages ago. I've matured
since then,' replied Sally. She was
standing with her hands on her hips.

'Yeah, right, Sally, you're so
mature that you still come to the tree
house,' I said.

After more heated discussion,
we decided that we would never
mention our tree house to anyone,
not even Shey. We didn't want
anyone else to know about it.

'Do you think you'll be scared

when we go whitewater rafting?' I asked Sally and Nathan.

'I might be a bit nervous,' Nathan said.

'How could anybody be nervous? Doing extreme sports is going to be a total rush,' Sally said.

I wasn't sure whether it was just nerves or whether I was really scared. But I know that every time I thought about what we were going to be doing, my stomach went a bit funny.

CAST AND CREW MEETING

On Friday afternoon, the limo
pulled up in front of my house to
take us to the cast and crew meeting.

The director told us that the
ratings for the first show were great.
'It's a ratings hit,' he said. 'We've
even started to get fan mail for you.'

They had made some posters of
us. We signed them as the director
talked. It all seemed a bit much to
me. A couple of weeks ago no one
even knew that we existed. Now

people were even going to stick posters of us on their walls!

'Over the next two days we're shooting on location at the King River,' the director said. 'Cars are on their way to pick us up and take us to the airport, so I'll have to keep this brief. Billy, Sally and Nathan, we have scripts for you to read on the plane. We'll do a read through first thing tomorrow morning and then we'll shoot your scenes. Of course, when you're actually on the river, you won't be reading from the script. You'll just be saying whatever comes into your heads. We'll have cameras positioned at intervals along the river, and a boat cam. You'll be wired for sound. Some of the crew will be staying till Sunday to shoot any location shots we need. Billy, Sally, Nathan and Shey will fly home Saturday night. Is that clear?'

Everyone nodded. The director grinned.

'So you'll be back in time to do your French assignments.'

Very funny.

As soon as the cast and crew meeting had finished, we left for the airport. The plane trip was terrific, except for the turbulence. The butterflies in my stomach flew out of my mouth. Lucky there was a paper bag in the back of the seat in front of me.

ON LOCATION

The next morning when we got to
the location, the crew were all there
waiting for us. All the female crew
were crowded around this one man.
Shey told us that his name was
Pierre. He was from France. He was
a world champion whitewater rafter,
and our special guest on the show.
Shey said that he was gorgeous. She
said that maybe he might like to be
on all our shows.

I thought that all the female crew

were talking to him because of his French accent. It did sound pretty cool. I knew then that I had found the best reason to try harder in my French classes.

# Location Map

## Our Equipment

**Wetsuit Boots**

**Life Jacket**

**Drybag**

**Straps**

**Rescue Bag**

**Whitewater Raft**

**Paddles**

**Helmet**

**Neoprene Gloves**

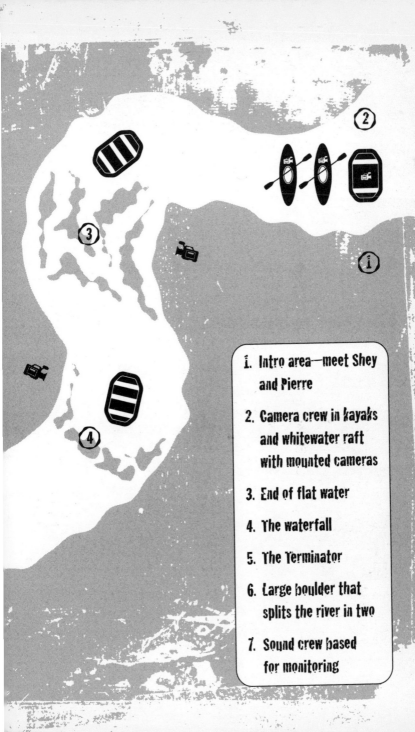

1. Intro area—meet Shey and Pierre

2. Camera crew in kayaks and whitewater raft with mounted cameras

3. End of flat water

4. The waterfall

5. The Terminator

6. Large boulder that splits the river in two

7. Sound crew based for monitoring

LIGHTS, CAMERA, ACTION

**BILLY**
Hi. Welcome to *The Xtreme World of Billy Kool*. My name is Billy Kool and these are my co-hosts, Sally and Nathan.

**NATHAN**
Today we're standing on the banks of the King River.

**SALLY**
We're about to do the first extreme sport of the series—whitewater rafting!

**BILLY**
With us is our safety co-ordinator and extreme sport expert, Shey. Hi, Shey.

**SHEY**
Hi, Billy, Sally and
Nathan. It's great to
be part of your extreme
world. Whitewater rafting
is a totally extreme
sport. Remember that
extreme sports can be
dangerous! You should
never attempt any extreme
sport unless you have
expert supervision and all
the safety requirements
are in place.

**BILLY**
That's why Pierre is with
us. Pierre is our river
guide and a whitewater
rafting expert.

**PIERRE**
Good morning!

**BILLY**
With your name and accent
it sounds like you might
be French. Is that right,
Pierre?

**PIERRE**
Yes, I am French. I come
from France!

**NATHAN**
Billy loves learning
French at school. You
might be able to help him.

**BILLY**
Yes, I'm trying to learn
French. It's a pity
my French teacher, Mrs
Crabtree, isn't here
today.

**SALLY**
Billy thinks that learning

French is a lot of fun!

**BILLY**
But not as much fun as
it will be going down the
rapids in a raft!

**SHEY**
This is our raft, which
is made of Hypalon.
Hypalon is a really sturdy
material and very hard to
put holes in. All the gear
we carry is lashed to the
gear frame with straps. We
are carrying drybags that
will stop the gear getting
wet if we tip over.
Thermal blankets and food
are kept in the drybags.
The thermal blankets will
help us get warm if we
fall in.

**NATHAN**
The food will keep our energy levels up and help to keep us warm.

**SALLY**
Nathan spends most of the day thinking about what he can put in his stomach.

**NATHAN**
There's nothing wrong with that.

**SHEY**
There's also a bailing bucket, in case we get some water in the raft. We also have a throw bag.

**BILLY**
Is that in case Sally starts to puke?

**SALLY**
I wasn't the one that
threw up on the plane trip
over here.

**BILLY**
That's just because of the
air turbulence.

**SALLY**
Yeah, right!

**SHEY**
A throw bag is also called
a rescue bag. It contains
a rope that you can throw
in case of emergency—like
if someone has fallen in.

**PIERRE**
It's good to see that
we're all dressed in
the right gear to go
whitewater rafting.

**BILLY**
We're wearing neck to
ankle wetsuits and wetsuit
boots that give us really
good grip.

**SALLY**
You look like a seal,
Billy!

**BILLY**
I'd rather look like a
seal than suffer from
hypothermia!

**NATHAN**
So what is hypothermia?

**SALLY**
That's what you get if
you fall into really cold
water and stay in it for
too long.

**SHEY**
The most important things
we have to put on are our
life jackets.

**BILLY**
Now we all look like seals
with life jackets on!

**SHEY**
The last things that we
have to put on are our
helmets.

**NATHAN**
Now we look like seals
with life jackets and
helmets on!

**PIERRE**
It doesn't matter what we
look like as long as we're
safe. I would hate to see
you get thrown out of the

raft and hit your head on rocks. If that happened, we might be talking about you in the past tense!

**SHEY**
We have the safety equipment on board. I think it's time that we got in the raft and started our extreme adventure.

*The camera crew have moved into positions along the river. The director gives more instructions. The cast get into the raft. PIERRE, at the rear, SHEY and BILLY on one side, and NATHAN and SALLY on the other side.*

**PIERRE**
Remember, I am the
guide and you have to
listen to what I say.
We are in still water
so we are going to
practise listening to my
instruction calls. Pick up
your paddles.

**BILLY**
The water is flat at the
moment, but I can hear and
see the water rumbling in
the middle of the river.

**SHEY**
Everyone listen to Pierre.

**PIERRE**
The calls are, 'all
forward'—that means we
all paddle to go forward.
'All back'—that means

that we all paddle to
go backwards. 'Back
left'—that means those
on the left paddle to
go back and those on the
right don't paddle at
all. The rest is easy
to understand. Now let's
try it. Right forward.
The other right, Nathan!
That's better.

**SALLY**
I've always said that you
don't know your left from
your right.

**NATHAN**
It's just that I'm a bit
nervous!

**PIERRE**
All forward. We'll paddle
to the middle of the

river and get into the main current. Alright, everyone, all forward. Let's get this show on the road.

**SALLY**
The raft is picking up speed. Can you see the white water?

**BILLY**
Yep, there's white water downriver. We're heading for some rapids.

**PIERRE**
That isn't a rapid. It's a waterfall. It's a three-metre drop.

**SALLY**
Can I get out of the boat? I'll meet you at the bottom.

**PIERRE**
The thing about paddling
in white water is that you
need to be looking ahead
all the time. Sometimes
you have to make split-
second decisions. When
we clear the waterfall,
we'll be going through a
narrow gorge with strong
currents. We'll hit
some rapids called 'The
Terminator'.

**BILLY**
It's a strange feeling
getting closer and closer
to the waterfall, but
not knowing what it'll be
like.

**NATHAN**
When do we just hang on?

**SHEY**
When Pierre tells us to!

**SALLY**
The raft is getting
faster. This is unreal.

**BILLY**
I think I can hear the
waterfall.

**PIERRE**
Keep paddling forward.
We'll be going really fast
in a moment!

**SHEY**
The waterfall is so loud!

**PIERRE**
Are we ready? All forward.

**BILLY**
Ready or not, here we
come.

*The camera crew is positioned at the top of the waterfall. They shoot the raft going over the edge. The raft bends and twists, then disappears from view as it plunges through the waterfall. Voices can be heard above the roar of the waterfall.*

**SALLY**
Aaaaaaaahhhhh!

**NATHAN**
Aaaaaaaaaaaahhhhhhhhh!
Watch out for the rock!

**PIERRE**
All back. Not forward,
Nathan!

*A boulder in front of the raft divides the river*

*in two. On one side of
the boulder, the river
races through a narrow
channel with a very strong
current. On the other
side, the force of the
water has created standing
waves half a metre tall.*

**SALLY**
Which way are we going?
Pierre? Which way?

**PIERRE**
Don't panic, Sally. Hold
on. All back, everyone.

*Pierre steers the raft
through the narrow
channel. The raft bounces
off the boulder. Everyone
holds on.*

**NATHAN**
I've got water up my nose.

**BILLY**
We've almost cleared the
terminator.

**SHEY**
Did you like it?

**PIERRE**
It's not over yet.

**SALLY**
I think I left my
stomach at the top of the
waterfall. That was crazy.

**NATHAN**
I'm glad I'm wearing a
wetsuit.

**BILLY**
Yeah, better than plastic
undies, hey Nathan.

**NATHAN**
Whatever.

**PIERRE**
All back. There's another
rapid coming up. Billy,
don't lean out of the
raft.

*The raft hits a rock and
tips up on its side. Billy
is dumped from the raft
into the water.*

**SALLY**
Biiiiiilllllllllllyyyyyyyy!

**NATHAN**
He's gone under!

**PIERRE**
All back. All back. We'll
pick him up. Here, Billy,
take my hand.

*Pierre hauls Billy back into the raft. He's shivering.*

**SHEY**
Are you alright, Billy?

**BILLY**
Brrrrr. The water's freezing. That was pretty hairy.

**NATHAN**
That's for sure.

**SHEY**
After these rapids we'll pull over and get the thermal blankets out of the drybag. We're nearly out of time for today's show, anyway.

**BILLY**
We're coming to the end
of our first sport. We'd
like to thank Pierre
for showing us just how
extreme whitewater
rafting is.

Just remember, if you
like to be extreme, then
extreme sports are for
you. Until next week,
on behalf of Sally,
Nathan and me, thanks for
watching *The Xtreme World
of Billy Kool*. I'm Billy
Kool and you're not.

**DIRECTOR**
Cut! That was fantastic.
Your little swim will make
great TV, Billy.

**BILLY**
Of course, that's why I
did it.

**SALLY AND NATHAN**
As if!

**BILLY**
Let's keep going. The
wetsuit kept me dry. I'm
starting to warm up again.
That was awesome.

**SALLY**
Let's go down some even
bigger rapids.

**NATHAN**
Why don't we just go down

the same rapids? It's not
like they were easy or
anything.

**SALLY**
You boys are chicken.

**BILLY**
If you're game to go down
the big rapids, so am I!

**NATHAN**
If Billy is, I am too.

**BILLY**
It'll be your turn to get
dumped.

**SHEY**
I think I'd better come
with you.

THE WRAP UP

That was totally awesome. I'm going to ask Dad if he'll take me whitewater rafting for our next holiday. Once we got started, the butterflies vanished. But my legs were a bit shaky at the end and my heart was beating so loudly I thought everyone would hear it.

Nathan and Sally seemed fine, but I wonder whether they felt the same way. Maybe they're good actors too. Maybe I should be an actor when I leave school. That's a great idea.

I'm really pleased that I met Pierre—he was cool. If I learn French, I wonder if I'll sound like Pierre when he speaks English. I wonder if Crystal likes French accents.

I can't believe that I fell in. On national TV.

**Dear Billy,**

My mum won't let me do any of the extreme sports that you have on your show. I want to do kart racing the most. Do you have any ideas about how I can change her mind?

**Joel, one of your fans**

# Extreme Information

# History

Rafting of some form has been around as long as there have been rivers and streams.

Rafts have always been used to transport people and cargo from one place to another.

Long before cars and trains were invented, rafts were used as a mode of transportation on the world's rivers and oceans.

The very first rafts were made of logs tied together with vines, or even animal skins. They enabled people to travel long distances for hunting and fishing.

Rafts also became very important for trading. People transported their goods long distances and traded with other river-goers long before railway systems were developed.

During World War II inflatable rafts, made out of rubber, were often used by the army to undertake commando raids and other dangerous missions. When the war ended many of these rafts turned up in army disposal stores. Families used these inflatable rafts as small swimming pools for their children, in their own back garden! But some adventurous people decided to try using the rafts on fast-flowing rivers.

They discovered that they could travel down rivers previously thought to be far too dangerous or remote. Because the design of the raft was shallow and very flexible, it was perfect for these wild adventures.

To help people decide which rivers to raft on, a grading system was introduced. This tells paddlers how dangerous (and difficult!) the various rapids are.

The rapids are graded on a scale of Class I to Class VI. Class I is just flowing water, with low risk. The most dangerous rapids are Class V and VI, and only very experienced rafters should attempt these.

# Glossary

**Dumped**

When you are thrown out of the raft and into the water.

**Eddy**

Where the water flows in a different direction to the main current behind a rock or other obstacle. An eddy can be a good place for tired paddlers to rest.

**Hairy**

Describes a very dangerous part of the river.

**House boulder**

A really big rock in the river.

**Hydraulic/stopper**

Where water flowing over a rock or other

obstacle flows downward and then back up over itself, creating 'white water'.

**Paddler**

A paddler is someone who 'paddles' a raft, canoe or kayak.

**Portage**

When you take the raft out of the water and carry it around very dangerous rapids or waterfalls.

**Put-in**

The start of a whitewater rafting trip, where the rafts are actually put into the water.

**Rapid**

When water flows quickly through a steep, narrow or shallow section of the river and causes 'white water'.

### River rating or class

Advises rafters of the difficulty of a rapid or river.

### Rock garden

A shallow area of river that has a lot of rocks.

### Run

A section of the river that is suitable for rafting.

### Take-out

The place where the rafts are removed from the water and the rafting trip ends.

### White water

When flowing water becomes frothy and white as it passes over rocks in the river bed, or through points in the river which are steep or narrow.

# Equipment

## Rafts

Whitewater rafts are inflatable boats usually made from laminated PVC or Hypalon, which is a very strong, flexible material. The largest rafts are usually about five metres in length and can hold eight to ten people. The smaller rafts hold two to four people and are about three metres long.

Most modern-day rafts are 'self-bailing'. This means that the design of the raft allows any water that spills in to escape without a paddler having to bail it out with a bucket. This ensures that the raft will not sink in very rough rapids where a lot of water gets into the boat.

## Paddles

These can be made from wood, strong
plastics such as fibreglass, or graphite.
For use in a raft the paddle will have a
blade on only one end of the shaft. For
a kayak the shaft may have a blade on
both ends. The blades are usually made of
plastic.

## Helmets

These are usually made from strong
plastic and lined with foam. A strap
beneath your chin holds the helmet in
place. The helmet will protect your head
from rocks and other debris if you fall
into the water.

# PHIL KETTLE

Phil Kettle lives in inner-city Melbourne, Australia. He has three children, Joel, Ryan and Shey. Originally from northern Victoria, Phil grew up on a vineyard. He played football and cricket and loved any sport where he could kick, hit or throw something.

These days, Phil likes to go to the Melbourne Cricket Ground on a winter afternoon and cheer on his favourite Australian Rules team, the Richmond Tigers. Phil hopes that one day he will be able to watch the Tigers win a grand final—'Even if that means I have to live till I'm 100.'

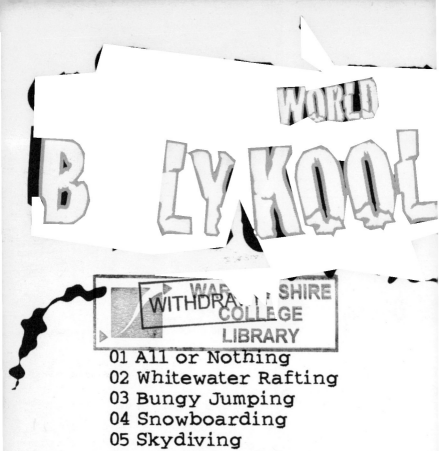

WORLD B LY KOOL

Billy Kool books are available
from most booksellers.
For mail order information
please call Rising Stars on
01933 443862 or visit
www.risingstars-uk.com